The Perfection of the Christian's Character, Consisting Particularly in Sincerity, Uniformity, Progression, Comfort, Agreement and Peace, Represented in a Sermon Preached ... Before the Assembly of Protestant Dissenters

The Perfection

OF THE

CHRISTIAN CHARACTER,

CONSISTING IN

Sincerity, Uniformity, Progreſſion, Comfort,

Agreement and Peace.

The Perfection of the Christian's Character, consisting particularly in Sincerity, Uniformity, Progression, Comfort, Agreement and Peace,

REPRESENTED IN

A SERMON,

PREACHED AT THE

Meeting-house, in Barbican, May the 26th, 1779,

BEFORE THE

ASSEMBLY

OF

PROTESTANT DISSENTERS,

OF THE

General Baptist Denomination:

By JAMES WALDER.

LONDON.

Printed for the AUTHOR, by J. BROWN, and fold by Mr. BUCKLAND, *Pater nofter Row*, and at the PRINTING OFFICE, *Fan Street, Horfly-down*, SOUTHWARK.

M DCC LXXIX.

ADVERTISEMENT.

ALTHOUGH every man, by the law of nature, hath an undoubted right to make choice of, and profefs what religion he pleafes, and to worfhip the Supreme Father Almighty, in what way and manner he thinks moft acceptable to Him, without the controul or interruption of any civil power whatever, yet I cannot omit this opportunity of expreffing my fincere gratitude and thanks to the worthy members of the Britifh Parliament, for the relief granted to diffenting minifters, by the late bill, now paffed into an act, which I confider and rejoice in, as a great enlargement of religious liberty.

As to the declaration, annex'd to the bill, I can readily and chearfully fubfcribe, not as believing, or acknowledging the magiftrates right to demand it, but as believing the matter and fubftance of the declaration to be true.

The Declaration ftands thus.

" I, A. B. do folemnly declare, in the Pre-
" fence of Almighty God, that I am a Chriftian,
" and a Proteftant, and, as fuch, that I believe
" that the Holy Scriptures of the Old and New
" Teftament, as commonly received in Proteft-
" ant Churches, do contain the revealed Will
" of God, and that I do receive the fame, as the
" Rule of my Doctrine and Practice. "

Oa

On making the above declaration before a magiftrate, and taking the oaths of allegiance and fupremacy, and making and fubfcribing the declaration againft popery, a diffenting minifter is entitled to all the exemptions and benefits of the toleration act, pafs'd at the revolution, and is deemed and conftituted a legal minifter, and is equally free and fecure from all penalties as a clergyman of the church of England.

May we all prize this day of great things, and ufe this liberty as not abufing it — May all diffenting minifters manifeft their firm attachment to, and real concern for the doctrines of chriftianity — And that all may live peaceable and quiet lives, in all godlinefs and honefty, is the hearty prayer of

The Author.

---

2 CORINTHIANS, x. 1, 11.

Be perfect, be of good comfort, be of one mind, live in peace; and the God of love and peace shall be with you.

THAT system of religion, which is properly called Christianity, delivered to us in the New Testament is an excellent institution; friendly to the very being, and interest of civil society — tending to advance our present comfort and prosperity — and conducive, in the highest degree, to prepare and qualify us for complete perfection and happiness in eternity.

The man, who enters into the real spirit and power of this divine institution, will have the ideas of his mind raised and exalted to the most noble and sublime objects — his affections will become purified moderate, and calm — his character and life will be adorned by an amiable and consistent conduct — and he will possess that inward peace and satisfaction which is not in the power of this world either to give, or to take away.

B 2   And

And, if this be the nature and defign of the chriftian religion — if it enobles our fouls — if it conveys prefent peace and ferenity to our minds — if it fpreads profperity around us, and tends to lay the moft folid and permanent foundation of happinefs, in the prefence and enjoyment of God, to all eternity, we ought to receive it with becoming attention and ferioufnefs of mind, and pay a due regard to all its doftrines and duties for, if we have any real concern, either for our beft intereft and fupport in this world, or, for the falvation and happinefs of our fouls in eternity, we muft have a concern for the fupport of the chriftian doftrines and duties.

We, — as a chriftian church — as difciples and fervants of Chrift — as children of God, and ftewards of his grace, are under tyes and obligations to fupport with zeal, refolution and fteadinefs the feveral important doftrines of that religion, which came from heaven, and we are to receive thefe important doftrines of the chriftian religion, and engage our felves in the duties of it, with a fupreme regard to the honour and love of God, and with a view that our minds may be impreffed and formed to the love and praftice of virtue and goodnefs.

St. *Paul*, in one of his addreſſes to theſe *corinthi-an* chriſtians, to whom the words of the text were ſpoken, intreats them, in the moſt affectionate man-ner, " to be careful not to receive the grace of God in vain ," and, in the words firſt read, which are his concluding addreſs to this church at *Corinth*, he expreſſes his ſincere and ardent deſire, for their complete and perfect eſtabliſhment in the chriſtian cauſe : " Finally, my Brethren, (ſays he) fare-" well — be perfect, be of good comfort, be of one ' mind, live in peace : and the God of love and " peace ſhall be with you."

This excellent inſtruction and advice, delivered by the Apoſtle to theſe primitive chriſtians, is equal-ly neceſſary to be received, and attended to by all chriſtians, in all ages, and in all the various cir-cumſtances of life. No chriſtian believer ought ever to ſay, he has no concern with, or nothing at all to learn from it · for, ſuppoſe our attainments to be very conſiderable in knowledge, faith and practice, yet we have ſomething to learn, and ſomething to do; and it muſt be our own fault, if theſe inſtructions are tranſmitted to us in vain.

But, as I am addreſſing myſelf to a collective body of chriſtians, who, I am perſuaded, are ſin-cere friends and advocates for the pure doctrines

and

and holy precepts of the gofpel, I fhall now beg leave, in all humility and love to fubmit to your candid attention an explanation and illuftration of the feveral diftinct parts of the text.

The FIRST Direction, recommended to us, is " Be perfect."

The Perfection here intended, I apprehend, may include three things.

Firſt, Sincerity

Secondly, Confiftency and uniformity of conduct.

Thirdly, A progreffive fteadinefs in the chriftian life.

Firſt, " Be perfect, " may include fincerity, for fincerity is a proper and neceffary perfection of human beings : it is a perfection, which, amidft all the infirmities and frailties of human nature, we are capable of attaining. Men may plead weaknefs and corruption of nature, but they cannot excufe themfelves from fincerity.

Sincerity is a neceffary perfection, or quality to every character in life — to the man of the world — the man of bufinefs — the mafter and the fervant — the rich and the poor — the high and the
low,

low, are all concerned in attaining to this perfection, and, above all, it is a neceffary quality apper-
taining to a religious charafter: It is that which
befpeaks dignity, and fpreads a glory over all the
private and public afts of religion; and the want
of this perfeftion will deftroy all the beauty, and
extinguifh all the value of every moral, or religious aft.

To affume the name and charafter of being religious, and, at the fame time, to be void of fincerity is to hazard our being detefted and defpifed,
whilft we are living; and, after death, to be expofed to future condemnation and perdition· fincerity,
therefore is a quality of the greateft importance,
and the higheft perfeftion of human nature; it is
that which will recommend us to the efteem and
confidence of men — to the approbation of our
own confciences — and to the friendfhip and love
God.

This perfeftion is attainable by every chriftian;
for, altho' we may not attain to any great honour,
or diftinftion in the world, on the account of our
abilities, or public fervices, yet we may all of us
attain to the honourable and amiable charafter of
fincerity in what we do. Every fervant of Chrift
— the weakeft as well as the ftrongeft — the mean-

eft

eſt and loweſt, as well as the moie honourable and uſeful may do their work, and labour in the feivice of religion ſincerely and "heartily as unto the Lord". They may all arrive to the perfection of ſincerity; every chriſtan may have a real and full intention, a fincere and hearty endeavour to diſ-charge his duty in all the branches of it, according to the abilities, means and opportunities he is poſ-ſeſſed of. and thus much, at leaft, muſt (I think) be included in the direction of the apoftle, " be perfect".

Whatever might be the firſt motive, or moving cauſe of our embiacing the chriſtan faith, and of entering into fo holy and honourable a profeffion, it ought now to be the leading view, the habitual and grand intention of our minds to be ſincere in what we do. Simplicity of difpofition and in-tegrity of fpirit muſt prevail throughout the whole of our religious engagements we muft not pie-fume to put on hypocriſy, diſſimulation and diſguiſe, when we engage our ſelves in the ſervice of our divine Maſter, but all oui intentions, thoughts and actions muſt be animated with ſincerity of love and reverence to God. " Be perfect," i. e. be ſincere, be in truth and reality what you profeſs to be — do not imagine that the mere name, or the external appearance and outward ſhew of
religion

religion will recommend you to the approbation of
God, and to your own confciences — fubftitute nothing in the room of uprightnefs of intention —
lay hold of no broken reeds — follow no cunning
deviled fables of men, but be ye the fervants of
God, and the Lord Jefus, in fincerity and truth.
The power and life of religion muft accompany
the form, and we muft have truth and fincerity in
the inward part.

Secondly, " Be perfect" may mean confiftency
and unformity of conduct; but abfolute perfection
is not here intended for, fo long as we continue to
be human beings, furrounded with the temptations
of the world, and the propenfities of nature, we
fhall not be wholly free from moral defects   Our
own experience and the word of God teach us to
believe, that to be perfect, in the ftrict fenfe of
the word, is morally impoflible, and therefore
this muft be far from the defign of the Apoftle's
exhortation in the text.

But to attain to a confiftency and uniformity of
character is a perfection which we, as moral being,
and free agents, are capable of, and fuch a perfection, or an uniform courfe of virtue the fcripture
repeatedly exhorted us to attain

And I perfume, there is great need for chriftian believers to be continually and earneftly warned and exhorted to the attainment of this perfection, to an uniform tenor of moral virtue, piety and goodnefs; for a flight review and examination into the conduct of men, will be a fufficient reafon and juftification for recommending this uniformity of behaviour.

Some chriftians with whom we are converfant, we learn, have faith, or fomething like faith — can give their affent to many of the doctrines of the gofpel — can converfe freely — and fpeak with fluency and fedatenefs on the principles of natural and revealed religion, but this their faith hath no proper weight, or influence on their conduct in life.

For, if we go with them into the world, and view them on the ftage of action, there we behold them in a habit, or drefs very unfuitable to their chriftian calling, and in a great meafure loft to manly, rational, and virtuous conduct.

If we travel with them to the field of commerce and bufinefs in life, we fhall fee, to our mortification, that their pretenfions to religion do not reftrain them from acts of fraud and injuftice.

If

If we follow them to the houfe of feafting, there we fhall fee them little concerned to fupport the laws of fobriety, moderation, and temperance.

If we attend them to the houfe of mourning, where objects of charity and diftrefs are frequently folliciting their help and beneficence; here alfo we fhall behold them deftitute of that chriftian fpirit, which giveth liberally and upbraideth not; their high pretenfions to admire the univerfal difplays of the divine goodnefs do not influence them to acts of mercy and charity. And, if this be the conduct of chriftians; if they act fo much below the excellent laws of chriftianity, and the moral character of the Deity, they ftand in need of being exhorted to a more perfect character, to be more uniform and confiftent in life.

If we are religious, only at certain times and feafons; — if our piety and reverence to God, and our love to virtue be eafily fuppreffed — if it be "like the morning cloud and early dew, which foon paffeth away;" — if its impreffions on the mind wear off, and we become cold and life-lefs in the moral and divine life, we ought to give the moft earneft heed to the exhortation of the Apoftle, to " be perfect" to act more uniformly, regularly, and confiftently, to renew our good re-
folutions,

folutions, and exert our chriftian courage, that fo we may exhibit an uniform character and example of piety, virtue, and charity.

Thirdly, The exhortation, "be perfect" may include a progreffive fteadinefs in the chriftian life. And this, I prefume, is no needlefs caution to a chriftian audience : for we are all, more or lefs, too inattentive to the culture and improvement of our minds, and too thoughtlefs and negligent in acquiring that wedding garment and furniture of the foul, which is a neceffary qualification for the kingdom of heaven.

Chriftians generally fpeaking, are more careful and diligent in acquiring a knowledge of the world, and in obtaining its riches, honours, and pleafures, than they are in acquiring a knowledge of human nature, and thofe religious and moral qualities of the mind, which are the higheft dignity and ornament to a rational creature : their attention to the world is fuch, that it befpeaks them children of error and darknefs, rather than children of light and knowledge ? And, while they are thus making unwearied endeavours to obtain earthly treafures, they abate and weaken their zeal, love and activity in laying up for themfelves treafures in heaven:

but,

But, if we are chriſtians by name, let us be ſuch in practice: let us remember, that we were born not for this world only, but for eternity alſo. Let us conſider human life in that true light, in which chriſtianity places it, as our ſeed time, and probationary ſtate; where, by a due improvement of our powers and privileges, we are to acquire thoſe pious and virtuous diſpoſitions and habits of ſoul, which will prepare us for the enjoyment of the divine and ſpiritual pleaſures of the heavenly inheritance. Permit me then to exhort you to go on to perfection — to make continued improvement and progreſs in the religious life — to run and be not weary — to walk and faint not — to preſevere with ſteadineſs and reſolution — to purſue religion as the principal thing, as the one thing abſolutely needful for our happineſs in eternity.

Let us bear it on our minds, that the chriſtian life is a progreſſive life, and, that as we have begun in the work of the Lord, we are to go on to a more mature, compleat and perfect ſtate · and may each of us be like St *Paul* — ' leaving the things which " are behind and reaching forth to the things which ' are before, preſs ſtill more and more towards the " mark, for the prize of the high calling of God, in " Chriſt Jeſus." I proceed to

The

The SECOND Direction, " Be of good Comfort."

The primitive chriftans were expofed to many fevere trials and perfecutions on the account of their faith in Chrift, as fuch the Apoftle gives them this advice, to take unto themfelves that confolation which the gofpel adminifters. They were to take comfort, and rejoice in the hope fet before them· their perfuafion of the truth of the chriftian religion, and the evidence which they now had of a future ftate, was to produce in their minds comfort under all their prefent fufferings and outward troubles : in all their afflictions they were to maintain an inward fatisfaction and ferenity of mind.

And this part of the apoftles advice has its ufe to chriftians at all times; for, altho' we labour not under fo fevere difficulties and trials now, as the firft chriftians did, yet we have all, more or lefs, our troubles and forrows: we labour under the frailties and diftreffes of a mortal life, are expofed to various afflictions and temptations, and under thefe we all need the comforts and confolations which religion and religion only can give. Religion is the great pillar and fource of comfort, it gives eafe and fpeaks peace to the mind under every outward diftrefs and misfortune. The good chriftian can look be-

yond

yond the troubles, evils, and preffures which attend frail mortality. He can extract confolation from the hope of a better world, to which he is raifed by the difcoveries of divine grace in the gofpel difpenfation. It is in the fchool of Chrift that the fincere believer can have relief under all his prefent difficulties and temporal diftreffes.

Our Lord himfelf has given a caution to all his followers, not to be over troubled, or caft down on the account of the fufferings and tribulations of the prefent life, and, in order that we may be fupported under them, and poffefs our fouls in peace and comfort, he recommends to us a belief in God, the Father Almighty, and in himfelf as the redeemer and faviour of men, " as the way, the truth and the life " and by whofe labours, death and refurrection, " we are begotten to a lively hope of an inheritance, incorruptible undefiled and that fadeth not away·" and it is by this hope, by the influence and power of this religious principle over the human mind, that we are enabled, amidft the fluctuation of all worldly things, to attain to that inward fecurity, reft and comfort, recommended to us in the text.

To " be of good comfort," may therefore be

D

confidered as an exhortation to chriftians to labour
after fuch a frame of mind, fuch a religious difpofition and fuch a relifh and veneration for virtue
and piety, as will yield an inward fatisfaction and
lafting joy. It is an exhortation to keep prefent
on our minds the great animating truths of religion,
and to live as thofe, who "have refpect unto the
recompence of reward" It is to maintain an habitual reverence to the laws, doctrines, and principles of the moral and fpiritual kingdom of Jefus
Chrift, by which we fhall obtain that ferenity and
approbation of mind, and that chearfulnefs and
comfort of foul, which can never be poffeffed by
men, who " live as without God, and without hope
in the world."

The exhortation, "be of good comfort," de-
mands our ferious attention and regard, on many
confiderations : for, — if our religious principles
and moral ftate do not yield this fruit, — if it does
not produce this internal peace and fatisfaction, it
is an evident fign, that our minds are too much fet
upon the things of this world, and our affections
alienated from God and goodnefs; and the lefs hope
and comfort we enjoy from the influence of religious principles, the lefs thriving and abounding fhall
we be in that piety and moral goodnefs, which will
recommend us to the divine favour: and if we are
not

not comfortable in our own minds, we cannot ad-minifter confolation to others.

Let us then be perfuaded to endavour after that religious furniture, which will inspire our minds with comfort, and render the journey of human life prof-perous and happy to our felves, and ufeful to others.

The THIRD direction the Apoftle gives to chriftians is, to "be of one mind."

This onenefs of mind here recommended, is of great confequence in the fcience of religion; as it will tend to revive, fupport and eftablifh that fpirit of zeal, love and veneration for it, which has been long complained of as being in a dying ftate.

The exhortation, is not to be fuppofed to mean, that we are to be juft of one mind, or fentiment in every point of religion. Our minds, like our bo-dies are differently formed, fome with more ftrength than others, and our ideas take their rife from diffe-rent objects, or from the fame objects through a different glafs; and as fuch they are fitted and de-figned for different offices in life.

" Having,

" Having, faith the Apoftle, gifts differing accor-
" ding to the grace that is given us ; whether pro-
" phecy let us prophecy according to the propor-
" tion of faith : or miniftry, let us wait on our
" miniftring : or he that teacheth, on teaching · or
" he that exhorteth, on exhortation · he that giv-
" eth, let him do do it with fimplicity : he that
" ruleth, with diligence : he that fheweth mercy,
" with chearfulnefs." All thefe different gifs, with
which God has endued us, are to be applied and
improved for the general benefit and mutual good
of each other. Let every one, faith St. *Paul*,
" pleafe his neighbour for his good to edification."
and we are exhorted " to bear one anothers bur-
" dens, and fo fulfil the law of Chrift. "

Firft, This onenefs of mind is, no doubt, intended to teach us to have a mutual concern for the
fupport, inftruction, comfort, and happinefs of
each other. That chriftian church, who are poffeffed of that onenefs of mind, which the Apoftle
recommends, will have fuch union of hearts, fuch
mutual friendfhip, and fuch concern for each other,
as to give and receive inftruction, in the fpirit of
meeknefs and good temper, and to exhort each
other with diligence, conftancy, and faithfulnefs;
and at the fame time ufe every motive to warn each
other from declenfions in religion. They not only
" give all

" all diligence, in making their own calling and
" election fure, and holding their own confidence
" and the rejoicing of their hope firm unto the
" end," but they have alfo a concern upon their
fpirits to bring others to diligence and perfeve-
rance in the religious life. They are not only diligent that they, themfelves, " may be found of
" Chrift, at his fecond coming, without fpot and
" blamelefs," but, alfo, are defirous that others
may ftand before him, with acceptance and ap-
plaufe.

This advice therefore, to " be of one mind,"
fhould teach and excite us to confult one anothers
prefent, fpiritual and eternal welfare. We fhould
each of us contribute our part to increafe the
knowledge, and promote the virtue of one another;
by doing of which we contribute to our joint and
mutual happinefs for this world, and that which is to
come. We are all probationers for an awful eternity, and nothing but moral and religious qualities,
through the mercy of God in Chrift Jefus, will fit
us for a friendly intercourfe with each other in the
future regions of immortality,

Secondly, This one-nefs of mind, may alfo include an exhortation to chriftian profeffors, to ufe

their

theii joint and united endeavours to eftablifh and promote the intereft of common chriftianity.

As all chriftians believe in the fame "God and Father of whom and by whom are all things," and are difciples of the fame mafter, and partakers of the fame bleffed privileges, hopes and promifes, they ftand in a fpiritual as well as moral relation to each other; from which religious connection and unity is derived an equal obligation to mutual endeavours to fupport that faith, which was "once delivered to the faints."

. We fhould be all united as brethren, as one family and houfehold, in " ftriving together for the " faith of the gofpel, ".— to be all as one body, " workers together with Chrift, " in promoting the honour of God, and the credit of religion. Be all of one mind, fo far as to be unanimous in maintaining the order, fimplicity, and purity of the gofpel law, faith and worfhip. Let the principles of religion have fuch weight and influence on each of our minds, as to unite us together in mutual friendfhip and love, for the defence of the truth.

And, I prefume, there is as much occafion now in the prefent age, to recommend this unity and' onenefs of fpirit in the defence of chriftianity, as

in

in the days of the apoftles, or in any fucceeding age The prefent time is alarming, on account of the degeneracy and corruption of morals, the increafe of infidelity, and the fpreading of the antichriftian fpirit of popery; all which have a natural and di-rect tendency to weaken, or leffen the number of rational believers.

It is an evil world, in which we live; we are in the midft of fnares and temptations, " evil men " and feducers wax worfe and worfe, deceiving and " being deceived:" and, need we, therefore, be told how much it concerns us, as proteftant diffen-ters, and as believers of the divine authority of the fcriptures, to adhere to the exhortation of the text — to " be of one mind " — to be united, as one harmonious body, in fecuring and fupporting that religion, which is from heaven, and is *firft* " pure, then peaceable, gentle eafy to be intreat-" ed, full of mercy and of good fruits, without par-" tiality and hypocrify." This leads me to

The FOURTH thing, recommended in the words firft read, *viz.* to " live in peace,"

This, truly chriftian fpirit, is what St. *Paul* had frequent occafion to recommend. He knew the
ftate

ftate of the world, and was well acquainted with the various and oppofite tempers of mankind; and, as frail imperfect creatures, he knew that a diffe‑ rence of opinion and intereft, together with the paffions of anger, pride and vanity, would often produce difcord, offences and quarrels: in fuch a ftate as this he faw how needful it was to recom‑ mend, with earneftnefs, a peaceable difpofition.

The primitive chriftians lived amongft men, who entertained an ill opinion of them, who either per‑ fecuted, or hated, or defpifed them; and this made it difficult for them to maintain, on all occafions, that humane, benevolent and peaceable fpirit which chriftianity teacheth.

Human nature is the fame now as heretofore: the malignant paffions of pride, hatred, wrath and malice ftill prevail among thofe who profefs the chriftian name and character; and it is from this fource, from thefe paffions and evil principles, that diffentions, cruelties, wars and fightings come a‑ mongft us: from the fame caufe proceed all pri‑ vate differences, family breaches and quarrels, for " where envying and ftrife is, there is confufion " and every evil work."

The

The gracious defign of chriftianity is to put an end to thefe evils, and to reftore mutual friend-fhip, peace and love amongft us. — " The Gof- *pel* " is one continued leffon of all the virtues con- " ducive to this end, and, if we had more of the " power of it, what a multitude of evils would " be prevented! How little of ftrife and animo- " fity would any where be feen! The provoca- " tions to it would be cut off.

" Divine inftruction is like a balm to heal " the fpirits of men, and as a band to unite " them. *

The exhortation, to " live in peace, " includes a difpofition to ' follow after the things which ' make for peace, and whereby one may edify " another." It implies a kind and friendly tem-per, behaviour and converfation, and a defire to cultivate a fpirit of humanity and love.

Man, by nature, is a fociable being, a creature made for fociety; and chriftianity teaches us to cultivate, cherifh, and maintain all that meeknefs,

* The above is a quotation, but I cannot recollect from whom.

E   mildnefs,

mildnefs, and tendernefs of fpirit, and that peaceable and gentle difpofition, by which we may contribute to the welfare, profperity, pleafure and
happinefs of civil and religious communities.

To live in peace is a defirable blefling; a blef-
fing on which many others are dependant. It is
defirable and important, becaufe highly intereft-
ing to private good and general happinefs.

By leading peaceable and quiet lives, in all
godlinefs and honefty, we contribute to the re-
vival of religion, and the flourifhing ftate of the
church of Chrift.

And, let it be remembered, that without cultivating a difpofition to live in peace, with our fa-
milies, with the feveral members of the church of
Chrift, and with all men, we cannot engage ourfelves in the duty of prayer, and other religious
fervices, either with pleafure or advantage.

" It is the God of peace whom we worfhip, it
" is is the Prince of peace, on whom we depend
" as our Saviour," it is by his word and example, that we are taught to live in peace; and,
by cultivating this moral and chriftian grace, we
are fitting ourfelves for admittance to the future
regions

regions of peace and glory, where nothing will enter to give us a moment's uneafinefs.

The LAST thing, from the words of the text, as a motive to engage us to maintain thefe moral and focial virtues, and to induce us to be confiftent and uniform in the chriftian life and charaƈter, is that " the God of love and peace will be with us," and blefs us.

The Apoftle teaches us to prefent the great Father of the univerfe to our minds, as " the God of love." and tnis idea of the the Supreme Deity, and a belief that he is the moral and merciful governor of the world, and the friend and rewarder of all them who diligently feek and faithfully ferve him, is the firft principle of religion, and the foundation for the fupport of piety and virtue.

We can read in the volume of nature, as well as in the book of grace, that " God is love," and it is a belief of the infinitely amiable perfeƈtions of his nature and moral charaƈter, that enables us to perform the duties of religion with delight, vigor, and conftancy: it is from this perfuafion that we are fupported with patience, fortitude, and calm ferenity, under the various affliƈtions of tne pre.

fent

fent life; and are animated with hopes of enjoying happinefs in futurity: and we may attain to a firm belief and certain knowledge, that the great parent of nature is goodnefs and love it felf.

His love and benevolence *is* vifibly infcribed in all the works of creation, — the effects and operations of his love and kindnefs are dayly and hourly exhibited before our eyes, in his government and providence over us—" his tender mercies are over " all his works," and thefe continue for ever, "with- " out any variablinefs or fhadow of turning. The " earth is full of the goodnefs of the Lord."

The evil and ungrateful are not excluded from it. " He caufeth his fun to fhine and his rain to fall, " on the juft and unjuft. Who then can be com- ·- pared with the Lord, he is wonderful in counfell," kind and gracious in all his dealings beyond all we can exprefs or concieve.

That he is the God of love, appeareth in that fcheme of falvation by Jefus Chrift, manifefted in the gofpel. Here we have a clear difplay of the divine grace and benevolence. It is a difpenfation of love, becaufe it is fuited to our prefent ftate, as frail, imperfect, and finful creatures; here we fee, that " God is love," and full of compaffion, defirous

of

of recovering all men from fin, and of raifing them
to holinefs, perfection and bleffednefs.

The gift of Jefus Chrift, as the inftructor, law-
giver and redeemer, is in the fcripture reprefented
as the effect of the divine love and goodnefs.

And if we are lovers of God "as dear and obe-
dient children," he will be with us and blefs us,
" he will be a fun and a fhield, and no good thing
" will he withhold from us." His providence will
be over us, and protect us. The friendly influences
of his holy fpirit will be with us, and comfort us.

If we continue to cultivate a religious temper,
to live chriftian lives and to be "ftedfaft immove-
able, always abounding in the work of the Lord,"
we may depend on God's direction. He will be
with us, and blefs us The word, the fpirit and or-
diances of the gofpel, will all, under the direction
of the God of love, be made fubferoient to our
comfort, and perfection in holinefs and happinefs.

He will be with us and befriend us with all needful wifdom, direction, and grace. He will care for
us, and fecure to us, every thing that is effential to
our real felicity; and he will conduct our fouls in
peace and comfort to his eternal kingdom.

Which

Which God, in his mercy, grant may be the happy portion of every one in this religious affembly, and all others who profefs themfelves the diciples of Chrift. Amen.

F I N I S.

Lightning Source UK Ltd.
Milton Keynes UK
UKHW022017270720
367264UK00003B/188